ACCOUNTING RATIOS
FINANCIAL RATIOS

Toye Adelaja

INTRODUCTION

Accounting ratio is a very useful tool for evaluating accounting figures and financial statements of a business entity. It is therefore, necessary to explain in details types and uses of accounting ratios. This book explained in details meaning, types, uses and calculation of accounting ratios.

TABLE OF CONTENTS

Chapters	Contents	Pages
	Introduction	4
1	Accounting Ratio	5
2	Types of Accounting Rtaios	7
3	Computation of Investment Ratios	10
3.1.	Earnings Per Shares	
3.1.2.	Basic Earnings Per Share	
3.1.3	Diluted Earning Per Shares	
4	Profitability Ratio	21
5	Liquidity Ratio	24
6	Long-Term Stability Ratio	27
7	Limitation of Accounting Ratios	28
	Appendix 1 (Practice Questions)	29
	Appendix 1 (Solutions)	33
	References	37

CHAPTER ONE

Accounting Ratio

1.1. Ratio

Ratio is used as a yardstick for evaluating the financial performance and financial position of a company.

The absolute accounting figures recorded in the financial statements cannot provide meaningful understanding of the performance and position of a business entity.

The relationship between two accounting figures expressed mathematically is known as Financial Ratio or Accounting Ratio.

Ratio makes it possible for users of financial information to get more understanding about the financial strength and weakness of a business entity.

1.2. Types of Financial analysis

There are many types of financial analysis. They are as follows:

1. Time series analysis: This is the method of analyzing the performance of a company by comparing the present ratio with the past ratio.
2. Industrial analysis: This is the comparison of a company ratio with the average industrial ratio fixed for all the companies operating in the industry.
3. Cross sectional analysis: This involves comparing the ratios of one company with some selected companies in the same industry at the same point in time.
4. Pro-forma analysis: This is the comparison of a ratio calculated from the financial information of a company with a projected ratio set by the company.

1.3 Uses of Accounting Ratio

The following are the various uses of accounting ratio

1) It is useful in predicting future performance of a company

2) It helps in inter-firms comparison

3) It helps to determine the efficiency with which a company is utilizing assets to generate income.

4) It helps in comparing past and present performance of a company

5) It helps to assess firm's ability to meet up with its financial obligation as at when due.

CHAPTER TWO

Types of Accounting/Financial Ratios

2.1. Types of Financial Activities/Ratio

The types of accounting ratios to be calculated are based on the intending uses of financial information. The following are the types of financial activities/accounting ratio:
   a. Profitability ratios and Efficiency ratio
   b. Liquidity ratio or short-term solvency ratio
   c. Long-term solvency or debt ratio
   d. Shareholders investment Ratios

2.1.1. Profitability Ratio and Efficiency ratio

Profitability ratio measures the performance of a business through profits. It is the ratio that is used to evaluate and access business ability to generate earnings having taken into consideration expenses incurred by the business. The higher the profitability ratio of a company, the more profitable the company is.

Efficiency ratio is the ratio that is used to measure how efficient the assets of a company are being utilized to generate profit. A major efficiency ratio is asset turnover ratio.

The common types of profitability ratio are as follows:
   1. Gross profit margin
   2. Net profit margin
   3. Operating expenses ratio
   4. Return on capital employed (ROCE)
   5. Asset turnover ratio

2.1.2.   Liquidity Ratio

Liquidity ratio is a financial ratio that is used to test a company's ability to meet and settle its short-term financial obligation as at when due.

A company should ensure that it does not suffer from lack of liquidity and does not keep excess funds. The inability of a company to meet its short-term financial obligations due to lack of sufficient liquidity will result in a poor credit worthiness, loss of creditors' confidence or even folding up of the company. A very high liquidity ratio is not good because idle asset will earn nothing.

The following are the various liquidity ratios:

1. Quick Ratio or Acid test Ratio
2. Current Asset Ratio
3. Cash Ratio
4. Stock Turnover Ratio
5. Accounts Receivable Collection Period
6. Accounts Payable Payment Period

2.1.3. Long –Term Solvency or Debt Ratio

Long-term solvency ratio measures the company's ability to meet its long-term financial obligation as at when due.

Long-term solvency ratios may be calculated from statements of financial position items to determine the proportion of debts in total financing. Long-term solvency ratios are also computed from statements of comprehensive income by determining the extent to which operating profit are sufficient to cover fixed charges.

Examples of long-term solvency ratio are:
a. Debt ratio
b. Gearing ratio
c. Interest cover ratio
d. Proprietary ratio
e. Cash flow ratio

2.1.4. Shareholders investment ratio

These are the accounting ratios which help equity shareholders and other investors to evaluate the quality and value of an investment in common stock of a company. The worth or value of an investment in common stock in a quoted company is its market value.

Shareholders' investment ratios are as follows:
a. Earnings per share
b. Earnings yield
c. Dividend per share
d. Dividend cover
e. Dividend yield
f. P/E Ratio

2.2. Standard of Comparison of Ratio for the Purpose of Financial Statement analysis

A single ratio is not meaningful enough to take decision because it is meaningless. One ratio cannot be compared with itself. A single ratio, in itself cannot be used to determine the financial strength or weakness of a business. It should be compared with some standards.

The following are the standards of comparison:
1. Past ratios: These are ratios calculated from past financial statements of a company.
2. Projected ratios are the ratios computed using projected financial statements of the company.
3. Industry ratios: These are the ratios of the industry to which the company operates and belongs
4. Competitors' ratios: These are the ratios of some chosen companies especially the progressive competitors which are in the same industry as the company under consideration.

CHAPTER THREE

Computation of Investment Ratios

3.   Investment Ratio

Investment ratios are used by shareholders and other investors to evaluate the performance of a business and to know the value of their investment in stocks of a company

3.1. Earnings Per Share

 It is necessary to explain in detail the earnings per share because is one of the most vital investment ratios available to investors. Earning per share (EPS) of a public limited company is regarded as a very important measure of a business performance. Earning per share is the income available to a unit of shareholding.

The price earnings (P/E) ratio is a fundamental stock market indicator and is based on the EPS. It is therefore important that EPS should be reported on standard basis for public limited liability companies.

There are two major types of earnings. They are basic earnings per share and diluted earnings per share.

3.1.2. Basic Earnings Per Share (BEPS)

It is the profit attributable to equity holder only. It can be computed by dividing Net profit after tax minus Preferred Dividend divided by number of shares outstanding during the period.

$$BEPS = \frac{\text{Net Profit after tax} - \text{Preferred dividend}}{\text{Number of shares outstanding for the period}}$$

3.1.3. Diluted Earnings Per Share

Diluted Earnings Per Share is the earning per share that has been adjusted for effect of potential common stocks. Diluted Earning Per Share is calculated to indicate to the investor the possible effect of a future dilution as a result of convertible securities such as convertible loans and convertible preferred stocks. The formula for calculation of diluted EPS is:

Diluted EPS = (Profit attributable to common stock holder + After-tax- interest on convertible debt + convertible preferred dividend) divided by Weighted average number of common stocks + All dilutive potential common stocks.

Diluted EPS will always be less than Basic EPS except there is no potential common stock.

Note:

Profit attributable to common stock holder is the same as Net income minus preferred dividend.

Important Note:

Anti-diluted Securities

When securities are converted into common stocks that will result in an increase in earning per share, the securities are called anti-diluted securities. Securities that increase earnings per share are ignored and should not be included in the calculation of the earnings per share.

Effect on the numerator

If convertible bonds are dilutive, then the bond's after-tax-interest expense would not be considered as an interest expense for diluted EPS.

Interest expense multiplied by (1-tax rate) must be added back to the numerator.

Effect on Denominator

Basic EPS denominator is adjusted for the equivalent number of common shares created by conversion of all convertible debt.

Formula for calculating diluted EPS where bond is convertible:

(Net income – preferred dividend)/Weighted average common shares outstanding + shares for conversion of convertible debts.

Note:
- Before calculating diluted EPS, one needs to check if the security is anti-dilutive

- To check whether convertible debt is anti-dilutive, calculate the following:

- Convertible debt interest (1-tax rate)/ Convertible debt shares.

- If the result above is less than Basic EPS, then the convertible debt is dilutive and hence, it should be included in the calculation of diluted EPS.

Example

During 2014 , Samotech company reported net income of $250,000 and had 100,000 shares of common stock. During 2014, Samotech company issued 1,000 shares of 10% par $100 preferred stock outstanding. In 2014 it issued, at par 600, $1,000 , 8% bonds, each convertible into 100 shares of common stock.

Assume tax rate is 40%

Compute the Basic EPS and diluted EPS.

SOLUTION

Basic EPS = Profit attributable to common stock holder
                Weighted average number of common stocks

            = $250,000 - $10,000
                  100,000

            = $2.4

The basic EPS is $2.4

Diluted EPS = (Profit attributable to common stock holder + After-tax- interest on convertible debt + convertible preferred dividend) divided by Weighted average number of common stocks + All dilutive potential common stocks.

The formula should be changed since there is no convertible preferred stock:

Diluted EPS = (Profit attributable to common stock holder + After-tax- interest on convertible debt) divided by Weighted average number of common stocks + All dilutive potential common stocks.

= $250,000 - $10,000 + $48,000(1- 40%)
      100,000 + 60,000

= $240,000 + $28,800
          160,000

= $1.68

Workings:

a) Interest on convertible debt

8% × $1,000 × 600 = $48,000

b) Calculation of convertible shares:

100 shares ×600 = 60,000 shares

Weighted Average number of shares

Weighted average of outstanding shares is a calculation that incorporate a change in the number of outstanding shares over reporting period.

Common stocks would participate in the earnings for the period of the year the shares are in issue. The weighted average number of shares reflects adjustments for additional shares issued and reacquired during the year.

Example

For example, if a company owns 100,000 shares on January 1 2010 and it issues an additional 100,000 shares on June, 2010, so the total amount of shares outstanding increases to 200,000. If at the end of the year the company reports earnings of $200,000, which amount of shares should be used to calculate EPS?

Solution

First half of the year 6/12 × 100,000   = 50,000shares

Second half of the year 6/12 ×200,000 = 100,000shares
                                                                  150,000shares

150,000 shares which is the weighted average number of shares should be used to calculate the EPS.

EPS = $\dfrac{\$200,000}{150,000}$

= $1.33

Adjusted Earnings per share

Adjusted earnings is the earnings calculated using the weighted average number of shares as the denominator. From the example above, the adjusted earnings is $1.33.

The following were extracted from the statement of changes in equity of Jendo International Ltd.

	2014	2013
	$	$
Net profit after taxation	24,960	21,940
Dividend proposed	-12,000	-11,500
Retained profit	12,960	10,440

An extract from the statements of financial position as at 31st December, 2014

	2014	2013
	$	$
Common stock of $1 each	50,000	42,000
Share premium	18,000	18,000
Capital reserve	22,000	22,000
Revenue reserve	32,000	25,000
	122,000	107,000
Non-current liabilities		
10% debenture	15,000	15,000
	137,000	122,000

NOTE: The market price of the company's share has been fairly stable at $4 per share.

Taxation for year 2014 and 2013 were $10,697 and $9,403 respectively.

Past ratios are used as the basis of comparison for the purpose of the following activities/stockholders' investment ratio.

Calculate the following investment ratios and make necessary interpretation

i.   earnings per share
ii.   dividend per share
iii.   dividend yield
iv.   earnings yield
v.   dividend cover
vi.   Price/Earnings ratio

SOLUTION
i.

	2014	2013

$$EPS = \frac{\text{Net profit after tax and preference dividend}}{\text{Numbers of ordinary shares}}$$

	2014	2013
EPS =	$\frac{\$24,960}{50,000}$	$\frac{\$21,940}{42,000}$
EPS =	$0.50	$0.52

Note: EPS = earnings per shares
      : Net profit after tax and preferred dividend is the profit available to common stockholder for distribution.

Earnings per share fell from $0.522 in year 2013 to $0.499 in year 2014. This shows that the performance of the company was better in year 2013 than year 2014.

ii.

The profit available to common stockholders are the profit after tax but the amount that they received is the amount distributed as dividend.

Dividend per share is a ratio that is used to evaluate the total amount of dividend payable per share issued. Therefore dividend per share can be calculated as follow:

		2014	2013
Divided per share			
=	$\dfrac{\text{Divided}}{\text{Number of shares}}$		
		$12,000	$11,500
=		50,000	42,000
=		$0.24	$0.27

The dividend per share decreased in year 2014 by $0.034 i.e. $(0.272 – 0.24). This reduction in dividend per share may discourage investors and make them to invest their funds somewhere else.

There are other two ratios that should be calculated when dividend per share is related to earnings per share. They are as follows:

a. Dividend cover = $\dfrac{\text{Earnings per share}}{\text{Dividend per share}}$

b. Dividend payout ratio is the reciprocal of dividend cover. It is calculated as follows:

Dividend payout ratio = $\dfrac{\text{Dividend per share}}{\text{Earnings per share}}$

iii.

Dividend yield is the return a stockholder is currently expecting on the stock of a company.

Dividend yield =

$$\frac{\text{Dividend per share}}{\text{Market price per share}} \times \frac{100}{1}$$

$$\frac{\$0.24}{\$4} \times 100 \qquad\qquad \frac{\$0.274}{\$4} \times 100$$
$$= 6\% \qquad\qquad\qquad = 6.85\%$$

The dividend yield for year 2014 was 6% and the dividend yield in year 2013 was 6.85%. Investors had better opportunity as regard dividend in year 2013 than in year 2014.

iv. Earnings yield evaluate the stockholders' return in relation to the market value of the shares

$$\text{Earnings yield} = \frac{\text{Earnings per share}}{\text{Market price per share}} \times 100$$

$$\frac{\$0.499}{\$4} \times 100 \qquad\qquad = \frac{\$0.522}{\$4} \times 100$$

$$= 12.48\% \qquad\qquad\qquad = 13.05\%$$

v.

Divided cover ratio measures the number of times in which the earnings available to common stockholders will be able to pay dividend declared.

$$\text{Dividend cover} = \frac{\text{Earnings per share}}{\text{Dividend per share}}$$
$$= \frac{\$0.499}{} \qquad\qquad = \frac{\$0.522}{}$$

$0.24			$0.274

=   2.08times   =   1.91times

The dividend cover for the year 2014 was 2.08times while that of 2013 was 1.91times. It showed that the investors and stockholders will be more beneficial in year 2014 than in year 2013.

vi.

Price/ Earnings ratio is the ratio that compares the current share price of a company to its earnings per share.

Price earnings ratio is the price an investor is paying for $1 of a company's earnings or profit. It is the reciprocal of earnings yield.

A high price earnings ratio shows that investors are expecting a higher earnings growth in the future compared to companies with lower price earnings ratio.

Price/Earnings ratio = $\dfrac{\text{Market price per share}}{\text{Earnings per share}}$

$$\dfrac{\$4}{\$0.499} \qquad\qquad \dfrac{\$4}{\$0.522}$$

= 8.016 : 1   =7.663 : 1

The price/earning ratio in year 2014 was 8.016: 1 and the price/earning ratio in year 2013 was 7.663: 1

Interpretation:

A high price earnings ratio shows that investors are expecting a higher earnings growth in the future compared to lower price earnings ratio.

Investors were expecting higher growth earnings in year 2015 than the earning they will be expecting in year 2014 because the P/E ratio in year 2014 was greater than the P/E ratio in year 2013.

Therefore, the P/E ratio of 8.016 in year 2014 was more favorable than P/E ratio of 7.663 calculated in year 2013.

CHAPTER FOUR

Profitability Ratios

The following formulas are used to compute profitability ratio:

1. Gross Profit Margin = $\dfrac{\text{Gross Profit}}{\text{Revenue}} \times \dfrac{100}{1}$

Gross profit margin shows the efficiency with which management manufactures or sells each unit of products.

A high gross profit margin may be a symbol of good and efficient management and a low gross profit margin may reflect high cost of goods due to management's ability to purchase inventory at favorable terms.

2. Net profit margin = $\dfrac{\text{Net profit}}{\text{Revenue}} \times \dfrac{100}{1}$

The Net profit, however, can be any of these:
   i.   Net Profit before taxation (NPBT)
   ii.   Net Profit after taxation (NPAT)
   iii. Net Profit before interest and taxation (NPBIT)

Net Profit Margin measures how effective a company is at cost control. A higher net profit margin indicates that costs are being minimized and revenues are being maximized. Net profit margin is a good standard of comparison of companies in the same industry.

3. Operating expenses ratios = $\dfrac{\text{Operating expenses}}{\text{Sales}} \times \dfrac{100}{1}$

Operating expenses comprise of distribution expenses and administrative expenses.

Higher operating expenses ratios are regarded as unfavorable because they will leave little operating income to meet up interest and dividend payments.

4. Return on Capital Employed = $\dfrac{\text{Return}}{\text{Capital employed}}$

The general formula for the calculation of Return on Capital Employed (ROCE) is mentioned above.

Return on Capital Employed is an accounting ratio that is used to measure the efficiency to which the capital of a company is used to generate profitability.

There are different formulas for the calculation of return on capital employed. However, the most important issue is to compare like with like so that there will be consistency between the numerator and the denominator.

If capital employed is defined as total assets minus current assets i.e. share capital plus Reserves plus Long-term Liabilities, then the return (Numerator) mean profit earned by all the capital. Therefore, the formula for this kind of return on capital employed is described below:

Return on Capital employed (ROCE) =

$\dfrac{\text{Net Profit before Interest and Taxation}}{\text{Shareholder's funds + Non-current liabilities}}$

A higher ROCE shows that capital is more efficiently utilized when it is compared to a lower ROCE. For example, where ROCE of two companies in the same industry are compared, the company that has higher ROCE is regarded as the company that utilizes its capital more efficiently than the company that has lower ROCE.

Return on Capital Employed (ROCE) is more appropriate for the comparison of the performance of capital intensive companies such as utilities companies and telecommunication companies.

CHAPTER FIVE

Liquidity or Short-Term Solvency Ratio

Types of liquidity ratio are as follows:

1. Current Ratio = $\dfrac{\text{Current Assets}}{\text{Current Liability}}$

Current ratio is used to measure a company ability to meet its short-term financial obligation. Examples of short-term financial obligation are short-term loan, bank-overdraft etc.

A current ratio of greater than one means that the company has higher current assets than current liabilities.

Current ratio is not the best ratio for the measurement of liquidity of a company because it does not measure the quality of assets. For example, where the assets of a company comprises of obsolete inventory and large amount of allowance for doubtful debts, then the company ability to redeem its debt may be difficult. It is therefore, advisable that too much reliance must not be placed on current ratio.

2. Acid Test Ratio = $\dfrac{\text{Current Assets - Inventory}}{\text{Current Liabilities}}$

Acid test ratio is a more reliable ratio that can be used to evaluate the liquidity of a company. Acid test ratio is also called quick ratio.

It is generally accepted that quick ratio of 1:1 is regarded as satisfactory liquidity.

3. Cash ratio = $\dfrac{\text{Cash + Cash Equivalent}}{\text{Current Liabilities}}$

It is generally accepted that cash ratio of 1:1 is satisfactory. Too much cash should not be kept and very low cash should not be kept by a company.

A higher cash ratio is not always good because cash should not be kept idle. A very low cash ratio is not good because the company may fail to meet its short-term financial obligation as at when due.

4. Accounts Receivable Collection Period

$$= \frac{\text{Average accounts receivable}}{\text{Credit Sales}} \times \frac{365}{1}$$

Note:
Average accounts receivable
$$= \frac{\text{opening receivable} + \text{closing receivables}}{2}$$

Average receivable collection period measures the speed of collection in days. The shorter period of collection indicates efficient collection period, while a long period of collection implies a very inefficient collection power.

5. Accounts Receivable Turnover $= \dfrac{\text{Credit Sales}}{\text{Average accounts receivable}}$

Accounts receivable turnover indicates number of times debtors turnover each year. The higher the value of account receivable turnover rate, the more efficient credit is being managed by the management.

6. Accounts Payable Period $= \dfrac{\text{Average accounts payable}}{\text{Credit Purchases}} \times 365$

Accounts payable payments period measures the numbers of days in which suppliers will be paid.

7. Stock Turnover Period $= \dfrac{\text{Average inventory}}{} \times 365\text{days}$

Cost of goods sold

Stock turnover period indicates the number of days that it would take a company to convert its inventory into revenue. The lower stock turnover period indicates a better management of inventory, while a higher stock turnover period indicates inefficient management of inventory.

8. Stock Turnover Rate $= \dfrac{\text{Cost of goods sold}}{\text{Average Inventory}} \times 365 \text{days}$

Stock Turnover Rate is used to measure the number of times in which inventory will be sold and replaced. The higher the stock turnover rate indicates efficient performance of the inventory management team.

CHAPTER SIX

Long-Term Stability Ratio

Debts ratio $=$ $\dfrac{\text{Total debts}}{\text{Shareholders' funds}}$

Debt ratio reflects the extent to which debt financing has been used in the business.

Gearing ratio $=$ $\dfrac{\text{Prior Charge capital}}{\text{Total Capital}}$

Gearing ratio is a ratio that is used to measure the proportion of debt to total financing.

The prior charge capital is the capital having the right to fixed income. Examples of such capital are:

i.   Debentures
ii.   Preferred stock
iii.   Long-term loan

The total capital consists of the following:

i.   Common stocks
ii.   Reserves
iii.   Prior charge capital
iv.   Minority interest (in group situation)

CHAPTER SEVEN

LIMITATIONS OF ACCOUNTING/FINANCIAL RATIOS

There are some limitations to financial ratios. The following are the limitations to financial ratios:

i. Financial ratios can only be used to compare the results of company having the same accounting policies. Financial ratio cannot be used to compare companies that have different accounting policies, otherwise wrong decisions would be taken by the users of accounting information.

ii. If effect of inflation is not considered in the calculation of financial ratio, misleading result will be arrived at.

iii. There is no stable standard that can be laid down for a perfect ratio.

iv. Financial ratio can only create an avenue for further investigation. It is not sufficient enough to make absolute final decision.

APPENDIX ONE

PRACTICE QUESTIONS

ACCOUNTING RATIO

1. One of the benefits of using accounting ratio is that they
A. are easy to calculate
B. facilitate decision-making
C. are stipulated by law
D. show errors and frauds.

2. Given
    Cost of sales $250,000
    Sales $320,000

The gross profit mark- up is
    A. 23% B. 28% C. 22% D. 15%

Use the following information to answer question 3 to 6.

	$	$
Sales		250,000
Opening stocks	?	
Purchases	100,000	
Less: Closing stocks	80,000	
Cost of sales	?	
Gross profit		?

The gross profit margin for the above information is 25%.

3. Calculate cost of sales.
A. $250,000 B. $187,500 C. $190,000 D. $120,000

4. Compute gross profit

A. $80,000 B. $62,500 C. $46,875 D. $18,000

5. Compute Gross profit mark-up
   A. 25% B. 30% C. 22.22% D. 33.33%

6. Calculate the opening stock.
   A. $167,500 B.$ 67,500 C. $187,500 D. $100,000

7. Calculate stock turnover rate
   A. 1.5times B. 2.5times C. 3times D. 6times

Use the following to answer questions 5 to 7

	$
Net profit	80,000
Total Assets	600,000
C urrent Liabilities	180,000
Current Assets	310,000

8. The current ratio is
   A. 1.72 : 1 B. 0.6 : 1 C. 1:2 D. 7.2 : 1

9. The capital employed is
   A. $150,000 B. $420,000 C. $310,000 D. $130,000

10. The return on capital employed is
    A. 61.54% B. 25.8% C.19.05% D. 1.72%

11. A low current asset ratio in a business indicates that the
    business is
    A. Able to use its resources efficiently
    B. Unable to pay its short-term bills as at when due
    C. Able to meets its short-term loan
    D. Keeping its assets

12. Which of the following best measure the ability of a
    firm to meet its short-term financial obligation?
    A. Current ratio B. stock turn over C. acid test ratio D.
    creditor payment period

Use the following information to answer question 13 – 17

The balance sheet extract of Jane Limited is given as follows:

	2009	2008
	$'000	$'000
Cash	1,130	-
Investment(marketable security)	860	750
Accounts receivables	5,030	5,350
Inventory	7,900	6,500
	14,920	12,600
Trade Creditors	-7,730	-7,150
Bank overgraft		-360
	7,190	5,090

13. Compute current ratio for the year 2009 and 2008 respectively.

A. 1.93 and 1.68 B.1 and 1.2 C.0.9 and 1.9 D.1.68 and 1.93

14. Compute quick ratio for the year 2009 and 2008 respectively.
A.0.98 and 1 B. 1.5 and 2 C.1 and 2 D. 0.91 and 0.81

15. Compute acid test ratio for year 2009.
A.0.91: 1 B. 0.81:1 C. 1 : 0.8 D. 2 : 1

16. Calculate working capital for year 2009 and 2008 respectively.
A. $660 and $750 B.$ 7,730 and $7,510 C. $7,190 and $5,090
D. $5,090 and $7,190

17. Compute cash ratio for year 2009.
A. 0.4: 1 B.1.2:1 C. 2: 1 D. 0.26: 1

18. The price-earnings ratio for a company with earnings per share of $4.32 is 11. If the total number of shares in issue is 60,000, what is the total market value of the share?

A. $2,851,200 B. $2,852,100 C. $23,564 D. $259,200

19. The ratio expressing the relationship between debt capital and
    equity holders" fund is called
    A. debt ratio B. interest cover C. proprietor ratio D. gearing
    ratio

20. Which of the following will be excluded from the calculation
    of acid test ratio?
    A. cash at hand B. bank balance C. inventory D. accounts
    receivable

    Use the following information to answer question 20 to 24.
    J.J. Ltd., during the current accounting period, had sales (all
    on credit) of $415,000 and cost of goods sold of $262,500. At
    the beginning of the year, its Accounts Receivable were
    $40,000 and its inventory was $50,000. At the end of the
    year, its Accounts Receivable were $43,000 and its inventory
    was $55,000.

21. Compute accounts receivable collection period
    A. 42 days B. 37 days C. 27 days D.40 days

22. Compute accounts receivable turnover
    A. 9 times B.11 times C. 13 days D. 10 times

23. Stock turnover rate is
    A. 5 times B. 7 times C. 73 times D. 1825days

24. Stock turnover period is
    A. 37days B. 73 days C. 83 days D.73 times

25. Victory company Ltd. has a debt-to-equity ratio of 1.9
    compared with the industry average of 1.5. This means that
    the company
    A. has less liquidity than other firm
    B. has higher credit worthiness than the industrial average

C. Will be able to meet its financial obligation earlier than other firms in the industry
D. has greater financial risk than other firms in the industry

APPENDIX TWO

SOLUTION

SOLUTION TO ACCOUNTING RATIO

1. B	11. B	21. B	31. D
2. B	12. C	22. D	32. C
3. B	13. A	23. A	33. C
4. B	14. D	24. B	34. C
5. D	15. A	25. D	35. C
6. A	16. C	26. B	36. B
7. A	17. D	27. A	37. A
8. A	18. A	28. C	38. D
9. B	19. D	29. A	39. D
10. C	20. C	30. B	40. A

WORKINGS

2.
$320,000 – $250,000 = $70,000
  Gross Profit mark-up = Gross profit/Cost of sales
                       = $70,000/$250,000 × 100%
                       = 28%

3.
Gross profit = 25/100×250,000 = $62,500

Cost of sales = Sales – Gross profit
$$= \$250,000 - \$62,500$$
$$= \$187,500$$

5.

Gross profit mark-up = $\dfrac{\$62,500}{\$187,500} \times 100 = 33.33\%$

7. Stock turnover rate = cost of sales/Average stock
$$= \$187,500/\$123,750$$
$$= 1.5 \text{ times}$$

8. Current ratio = $\dfrac{\text{current asset}}{\text{current liability}}$ = $\dfrac{\$310,000}{\$180,000} = 1.72$

9. Capital employed = Total assets – Current liabilities
$$= \$600,000 - \$180,000 = \$420,000$$

10.Return on capital employed = $\dfrac{\text{Net profit}}{\text{Capital employed}} \times 100\%$
$$= \dfrac{\$80,000}{\$420,000} \times 100\%$$
$$= 19.05\%$$

14. Quick ratio = $\dfrac{\text{Current assets- inventory}}{\text{Current liability}}$

	2009	2008
Quick ratio =	$\dfrac{\$14,920 - \$7,900}{\$7,190}$	$\dfrac{\$12,600-\$6,500}{\$7,510}$
=	0.98	0.81

15.Acid test ratio is the same as quick ratio. 0.98: 1

16. Working capital = Current Assets – Current Liabilities

17, Cash ratio = $\dfrac{\text{cash + cash equivalent}}{\text{Current Asset}}$

$$= \frac{\$1,130 + \$860}{\$7,730} = 0.26$$

18. Price-earnings ratio $= \dfrac{\text{MPS}}{\text{EPS}}$

$\dfrac{\text{MPS}}{\$4.32} = \$11$

MPS = $47.52

Total market value of the share = $47.52×60,000 = $2,851,200

NOTE: MPS = Market price per share, EPS = Earning per share

21. ARCP $= \dfrac{\text{AVAR}}{\text{SALES}} \times 365\text{days}$

$= \dfrac{\$(40,000 + 43,000)/2}{\$415,000}$

$= 37\text{days}$

NOTE: ARCP = Accounts Receivable Collection Period

AVR = Average Accounts Receivable

22. Accounts receivable turnover $= \dfrac{\text{Sales}}{\text{AVAR}}$

$= \dfrac{\$415,000}{\$41,500}$

$= 10\text{times}$

23. Stock turnover rate $= \dfrac{\text{COS}}{\text{AVS}}$

$= \dfrac{\$262,500}{\$(50,000 + 55,000)/2}$

$= 5 \text{ times}$

NOTE: COS = Cost of sales,   AVS = Average stock

24. Stock turnover period $= \dfrac{\text{AVS}}{\text{COS}} \times 365 \text{ days}$

$= \dfrac{\$(50,000 + 55,000)/2}{\$262,500}$

$= 73 \text{ days}$

REFERENCES

ICAN Study Pack (FA II)

Toye Adelaja (2015) – Basic Financial Accounting (MCQ & A)

Toye Adelaja (2015) – Financial Statements Analysis

www.accoutninghour.com